Morton's College Student Dictionary

Morton's College Student Dictionary

First Edition

Carl E. Morton

iUniverse, Inc.
New York Lincoln Shanghai

Morton's College Student Dictionary
First Edition

Copyright © 2005 by Carl E. Morton

iUniverse books may be ordered through booksellers or by contacting:

iUniverse
2021 Pine Lake Road, Suite 100
Lincoln, NE 68512
www.iuniverse.com
1-800-Authors (1-800-288-4677)

ISBN: 0-595-33743-0

Printed in the United States of America

I dedicate this book to my mother, Bessie Morton, for a lifetime of love and support. Thank you.

MORTON'S COLLEGE STUDENT DICTIONARY

-A-

A (+/-): wishful thinking for the B-students.

A++: 100% and the extra credit question.

A-effort: to give it the old college try; regardless of the actual grade you receive.

A-student: someone who is right 95% of the time.

AAA (*triple A*): an excellent report card.

ABC's: three of the many possible options on a multiple-choice question.

abroad: to study way off campus for a semester.

absent: missing in action.

academic calendar: the school year at a glance.

academic freedom: being able to choose your own major.

academic probation: when your parents threaten to not pay tuition if your grades don't improve.

academics: the quality of the education you're getting...or not getting.

academic standing: whether you're a freshman, sophomore, junior or senior.

academic year: the 9 months that school is in session.

aced: you came, you saw and you conquered the exam.

add: to voluntarily increase your workload for the semester.

add/drop: the course exchange-program.

ad-lib: academic improvisation.

admissions: the selective process of rejecting prospective students.

advisor: an upperclassman friend who has the same major.

AI (*artificial intelligence*): getting an A because you cheated.

aisle seat: making good use of the floor in an overcrowded classroom.

afterthought: remembering the answer to a question after the exam is over.

alarm clock: a boom-box that tells time.

All-American: a college lacking enrollment of a single international student.

all-nighter: to study from dusk 'til dawn...and then some.

alma mater: old school.

alphabetical: the order professors are likely to distribute graded work.

alphanumeric: getting both a letter grade and a score.

alumni: your campus predecessors.

AM (*Almost Monday*): the "Sunday night blues" in anticipation of going to classes in the morning.

analyze: to think long and hard about something.

answer: a spoken or written response...that may or may not be correct.

answering machine: the know-it-all sitting in the front row.

answering service: the roommate of a very popular student.

answer sheet: a blue book.

anti-virus: a flu shot.

AOTA (*all of the above*): a guess as good as any when you don't know the answer on a multiple-choice question.

AP (*advanced placement*): upperclassmen need only apply.

Arts & Sciences: the difference between a BA & a BS.

assignment: home work.

Associate Degree: ½ a BA.

Associate professor: a co-teacher.

attachment: how to submit your paper for a grade.

attendance: class participation.

audit: to take a dry run of a course.

auditorium: a lecture hall.

AWOL (*absent...was out late*): a popular excuse for skipping your early morning class.

-B-

B (+/-): good, but no cigar.

B-student: someone who is right 85% of the time.

BA: the difference between earning a degree in *Arts* vs. sciences.

baccalaureate: a fancy term for bachelor's degree.

bachelor's degree: a pre-requisite to a graduate degree.

backfill: to answer all of the test questions that you previously left blank.

backpack: getting everything you brought to campus ready for the return trip home.

bad hair day: why you should have at least one baseball cap in your wardrobe.

B&B (*bed and breakfast*): housing and a very limited meal plan.

bed: a twin-size dorm room sleep-sofa.

bed head: a clear sign that someone didn't shower.

bed lamp: a college student's night light.

bedtime: whenever you succumb to the need for sleep.

beer: the traditional beverage of choice for college party goers.

bilingual: what every student majoring in a language aspires to become.

black board: the classroom dry-erase board.

blank: a student's expression when asked a question about which he/she has no idea.

blue book: the universal color-coded, test-taking answer sheet.

BMOC (*big man on campus*): the school's very own celebrity.

BO (*body odor*): possibly why there remains an empty seat next to one student, in an otherwise overcrowded classroom.

board: a meal plan.

bombed: to get way more wrong than right.

book(s): required reading material.

book bag: whatever you happen to carry your books in.

book cover: using your textbook to hide the magazine that you are actually reading.

book expense: the total cost of your required reading for the semester.

booklist: an inventory of all your required reading for the semester.

bookmark: that fold you made in the corner of the page.

book notes: whatever the previous book owner wrote on the pages.

book report: your interpretation of a literary work.

book smart: a devoted scholar…lacking common sense.

bookstore: the campus souvenir shop.

bookworm: a Saturday night regular at the library.

borderline: an answer or two away from failing.

bored: the sensation you get when there is nothing to do but study.

borrow: what precedes an I-O-U.

borrowed time: however long your classmate gives you to copy their notes and return the notebook.

boxers: unisex underwear.

boycott: a no-class action suit.

brain freeze: when you absolutely know the answer, but you just can't seem to remember it.

brainstorm: having studied so much that you can't think straight.

breakfast: the early bird special at the dinning hall.

BS: the art of what you've learned to master by the time you graduate. *bull sh-t.*

brownnose: to actively engage in being a teacher's pet.

buddy list: everyone that you'd invite if you were throwing a party.

bulletin board: where post-it notes go.

bunk beds: space saving dorm room design. Some assembly may be required.

bunk mate: the person who regularly sleeps directly above/below you.

bursar's label: your tuition receipt.

bursar's office: the college collection department.

business: what a nosey roommate won't mind of their own.

buy back: the bookstore return policy.

BYOB (*Bring Your Own Book):* classroom etiquette, so that you can follow along.

-C-

C (+/-): par for the course.

C-student: someone who is right 75% of the time.

cafeteria: the campus lunchroom.

campus: the school zone.

campus map: a freshman guide to where everything is.

cancellation: a registration hazard when apparently you were the only one interested in taking the course.

cap & gown: the ceremonial school uniform.

care package: a special delivery.

case study: the obsessive personality of your crazy roommate.

catch-up: a concerted effort to get to where the syllabus says you already are.

CD's: not the grades that you'd prefer to see on your report card.

CD collection: a transcript full of mediocre & poor grades.

cell phone: a student's lifeline.

chapter(s): what you've been assigned to read for the next class.

chat room: the lounge area at the student center.

cheat: good grades by any means necessary.

cheat sheet: a note to self.

checkmark: confirmation that you were right.

chemistry: the compatibility, or lack of, between room-mates.

class: what some students lack no matter how many courses they take.

class act: to pretend that you're paying attention to the lecture.

classmate: someone from whom you might borrow notes.

class participation: raising your hand every now and then.

classroom: the designated course rendezvous point.

class size: the most obvious difference between a seminar and a lecture course.

class time: the number of hours per week that you're suppose to be in class.

cliff notes: the truly abridged version of a book.

clique: an impenetrable study group.

clockwise: knowing exactly which classroom clocks keep accurate time.

closed: a registration hazard when apparently you were far from the only one interested in taking the course.

closet: a dorm room of very limited size.

club: a fail-safe sandwich option in the dining hall.

co-ed: his & hers.

cold calling: the random student selection process by which professors check to see who has done the reading.

college: a 4 year deferment into the real world.

collegiate: anything that has anything to do with college.

commencement: the beginning of the rest of your life.

common sense: what some students lack no matter how many A's they get.

community college: a commuter school.

commute: frequent travel mileage to and from campus.

comprehend: to actually understand what you just read.

consciousness: awake time in between classes.

copier: a plagiarist.

copy: how you plan to get the notes for the day(s) that you missed class.

copy right: making sure that you take accurate notes.

core courses: what no major is complete without.

correct: the professor's obligation to grade your work.

course: the road to earning your degree.

course catalog: the inventory of classes available at the college.

course description: feedback from someone who has already taken the class.

course listing: a student's guide to scheduling.

course load: the total combined weight of all your books for the semester.

course material: subject matter.

coursework: everything you're assigned to complete for the semester.

cram: the attempt to learn a semester's worth of information in just a few days.

crash course: the one class that you did poorly in.

creative writing: trying to answer an essay question about which you have minimal knowledge.

credit: getting approved for a student Visa or MasterCard account.

credit hours: the true value of a course.

critical thinking: having to get the answer right…or else.

cross reference: to compare your answers by asking classmates what they got.

cum laude: Latin for 'grades above the call of duty.'

cumulative: an exam on everything covered in the class from day one.

cumulative average (aka *cum*): the sum of all your grades.

curriculum: everything listed in the course catalog.

curve: a graphic representation of how much better grades are with extra points added on.

curve-buster: a straight A student.

cyber space: where that unsaved document disappeared to.

-D-

D: a clear indication that you didn't study enough.

D-day: any day on which you receive a poor grade.

D-student: someone who is right 65% of the time.

daydream: to imagine that you are anywhere other than in class.

dead line: an assignment expiration date.

dean: the school official for whom a list is compiled in their honor.

dean's list: the honor roll.

debate: an argument between roommates.

deductive reasoning: trouble shooting.

degrade: one full mark worse than a C grade.

degree: what every student hopes to have earned when all is said and done.

degree program: a major course of study.

degree requirements: to earn all of the credits necessary to complete the program.

de ja vu: getting the same grade that you got on the last exam.

desk: standard dorm issued workstation.

desk lamp: a work light.

desk mat: a giant notepad.

dictionary: a good, old-fashioned spell checker.

dining hall: where students go for their servings of 3 square meals a day.

dining services: the campus caterer.

dinner: last call at the dining hall.

diploma: your graduation receipt.

directions: step by step instructions on how to find a building/location on campus.

disciplinary probation: when your parents threaten to not pay tuition if you don't behave yourself.

discredit: when a college fails to recognize a course taken at another school.

disorientation: getting lost on campus.

distribution requirement: to take one hand-out and pass the others back.

divine intervention: the postponement of an exam that you were not ready to take.

DNA (*did not attend*): absent.

DOA (*dead on arrival*): appearing to take an exam that you know you have no chance of passing.

doctor: a high ranking professor.

doodling: drawing when you should be taking notes.

dormer: a student living in a dormitory.

dormitory (aka *dorm*): a campus rooming house.

dorm room: your home away from home for the school year.

dorm room accessories: all the comforts of home.

double: standard size dorm room accommodations.

double check: to go over your work again, just to be sure.

double major: 2 degrees for the price of 1.

double space: how to turn a 7 page paper into a 10 page paper.

double standard: the housing policy that dictates assigning 2 students to a room.

double take: having to repeat a course that you previously did poorly in.

downgrade: anything less than you got on the previous exam.

download: to drop a course.

drool: an obvious sign that your classmate is asleep.

drop: a registration annulment.

drop out: the ultimate incomplete.

due date: when you're supposed to return that book to the library.

-E-

early bird special: the option to sit wherever you want in class…because you're one of the first to arrive.

easy: a professor and/or a course that poses no academic challenge whatsoever.

economics: sound financial reasoning for buying used books.

edit: to cut and paste.

education: what you're paying all of that money for.

electives: any course of your choice outside of your major.

email: correspondence delivered in 2–4 seconds.

email address: your online alias.

engineering: the logical major for an aspiring train conductor.

escape (*Esc*): to sneak out of class before it's officially over.

escort: whomever you walk to class with.

essay: the writing section of an exam.

ET Syndrome: a freshman's uncompromising urge to call home.

evacuation day: the mass exodus from campus at the end of the school year.

exam: a questionnaire worth a large percent of your final grade.

example: a demonstration of how it's suppose to be done.

exam sheet: the actual test questionnaire.

exchange program: the option to switch your major.

exchange student: what you would like to do with an annoying roommate.

excuse: any story explaining why you don't have your homework.

expulsion: a dishonorable discharge from a college.

extension: another day or two to complete an assignment.

extra-credit: getting another student Visa or MasterCard.

-F-

F: a clear indication that you didn't study at all.

F-bomb: a normal reaction upon getting a failing grade.

facilitator: the difference between a debate and an argument.

faculty: everyone authorized to teach at the school.

faculty-student ratio: the average class size if everyone had class at the same time.

fad: something that was popular yesterday.

FAF: a terrible report card.

fail: 59% or worse.

fall: the first semester of the school year.

false: possibly the correct answer on a True/False question.

false alarm: being awakened early by your roommate's clock.

FAQ's (*frequently asked questions*): Should I go to class today? Can I borrow your notebook? When is the assignment due?

fast food: anything microwave able.

fee: the cost, per page, to have someone type your paper.

fiction: creative writing.

final(s): the semester's main event.

financial aide: the student discount towards the cost of tuition.

financial aide form: the student discount application.

financial aide office: the student discount processing center.

fire drill: wishful thinking when taking a tough exam.

first class: whichever course starts your day.

5mm (*five more minutes*): wishful thinking whenever the time limit has expired and you're not quite done.

floor: where you are instructed to place your belongings prior to taking an exam.

flunk: to get too many wrong.

formula: a recipe for getting the right answer.

foot locker: a dorm room coffee table.

footnote: kicking a classmate under the table.

four point O (4.0): an outdated version of Aol.

fraternity (aka *frat*): an exclusive boys only club on campus.

fraternity house: an exclusive boys only clubhouse on campus.

freshman: low man on the campus totem pole.

Freshman 15: a popular first year student diet plan.

freshman year: the inaugural college experience.

Friday: day 5 of classes for the week and the official start of the weekend.

friends: dinning partners.

front row: reserved seating for the smart students and/or late arrivals to class.

Frosh: slang for "low man on the campus totem pole."

FYI (*for your information*): everything that a professor mentions in class.

-G-

geography: the campus landscape.

ghost writer: the author of those reports available for sale on the internet.

glossary: the list of vocabulary words at the back of the book.

gossip: he said, she said.

GPA (*grade point average*): your academic IQ.

grade(s): the fruit(s) of your labor.

grading system: how professors rank the students in a class.

graduate: what every student aspires to become.

graduate school (aka *grad school*): post college deferment into the real world.

graduate student: someone for whom 4 years of college wasn't quite enough.

graduation: the ceremonial rite of passage into the real world.

Greek: the alphabet used to distinguish fraternities & sororities from one another.

guess: an alternative to leaving the answer blank.

gut: a course that requires minimal effort to ensure a good grade.

-H-

hacker: a classmate badly in need of a cough suppressant or a drink of water.

hall: a campus building named in honor of a generous donor to the college.

hall mates: your dorm neighbors.

hand-out: an addendum to the daily lesson.

handwriting: a resourceful solution when you have a pen and no paper.

hang out: a popular students' dorm room.

hangover: a college party-favor.

hard: a professor and/or a course notorious for giving students a run for their money.

hard cover: the difference of about $50 in the cost of a book.

heavy sleeper: a student immune to alarm clocks.

hiatus: to take a semester or two off.

hieroglyphics: extremely poor handwriting.

higher education: the pursuit to learn more than you already know.

high-light: to color in your textbook.

high-lighter: a book-marker.

high school: college prep.

hike: the long walk to get to class at the other end of campus.

hindsight: knowing now what you should've known before the exam.

hint: a clue as to what will be on the test.

history: any chance you have to earn an A once you've failed the mid-term.

holidays: the source of long weekends.

home: a popular student weekend retreat.

homecoming: the prodigal child's return home at the end of the school year.

home schooling: when your parents play professor.

homesick: the longing to return to campus after spending just few hours visiting home.

hometown: the big city closest to where you actually live.

homework: a little something to tide you over until the next class.

honorable mention: almost making the dean's list.

honorary degree: an academic consolation prize.

honors: anything with the words 'cum laude' after it.

honor system: student self policing.

hooky: a planned absence.

housemates: off campus roommates.

housing: the difference between a short walk to class and a long commute.

housing lottery: whatever the odds are that you'll be matched with a compatible roommate.

hypothesis: something to prove.

hypothetical: what if?

-|-

I: a grade reminder that there is still work to be done.

ID card: your freshman photo laminated for posterity.

IDs (*identifications*): the make or break section of an exam.

IEP (*Individual Education Plan*): an outline of what classes you'll take, in which semester and during which year.

incomplete: a work in progress.

independent study: to prepare for the exam all on your own.

instant messaging: the personal notes passed between classmates during class.

in state: college not too far from home.

instructions: how it's done.

instructor: one who is certified to show you how it's done.

international student: someone studying abroad.

international relations: dating someone from another country.

internet: the ability to do research at the click of a button.

internet provider: your college.

internship: field work.

intramurals: organized pick-up games.

introductory level: any course listing with the number 101.

IOU: a promissory note.

-J-

journal: a written documentary of the semester.

junior: heir to the campus throne.

junior college: where you go to earn an associates degree.

junior year: the next to last go around on campus.

-K-

keg: the traditional college party guest of honor.

keynote: that caveat of information that you just know is going to be on the exam.

keynote speaker: your professor...especially during the last class before the exam.

keynote address: the last class before the exam.

knapsack: a book bag which doubles as a pillow during class.

know: to retain information...even after the exam is over.

know-how: what you'd best have in order to complete the assignment.

know-it-all: a straight A student.

-L-

Labor Day weekend: the unofficial start of the school year.

languages: foreign studies.

lap top: the retractable piece of wood attached to each chair in the lecture hall.

last minute: a procrastinator's starting point.

late: to arrive anytime after the lecture has begun.

late night: the wee hours of the morning.

late sleeper: a student whose schedule shouldn't contain any morning classes.

laundry: the clothes that absolutely should not be worn again before washing.

learn: to read and actually comprehend the material.

learning curve: the number of class sessions between exams.

lecture: words of wisdom from your parents regarding mediocre or poor grades.

lecture course: a great big class.

lecture hall: a great big classroom.

leftovers: the remaining courses available to choose from when you register late.

lesson: whatever it is that you just learned and then told yourself that you won't ever do again.

Liberal arts: to learn a little about a lot.

Liberal arts degree: certification that you know a little about a lot.

library: your personal collection of books accrued over 4 years of college.

light sleeper: a student who routinely goes to bed with the light on.

light year: back to back semesters of minimal course-work.

line: what you're sure to be standing in while waiting to register.

literature: reading material.

Lit (aka *literature*): a course description forewarning of extensive reading and writing.

loan: what precedes a U-O-ME.

long weekend: having to study your butt off for an exam scheduled on Monday.

ost & found: your understanding of subject matter before & after you get a tutor.

lunch: breakfast for the majority of students.

-M-

Magna cum laude: Latin for 'grades above and beyond the call of duty.'

mail: correspondence delivered in 2–4 days.

mail-order: a student's demand on their friends to write.

major: your academic specialty.

make-up: a second-chance to complete a missed exam/assignment; pending your professor' approval.

margins: reserved space for your professor's comments and corrections.

mark down: the automatic grade reduction for each day that your assignment is late.

mascot: the campus clown.

materials fee: the cost of school supplies.

matriculation: the daily flow of students across campus.

meal plan: who you're eating with, at what time and in which dining hall.

memorize: to learn by heart...in preparation for the exam.

mental note: a conscious effort to remember something without having to write it down.

message board: a dorm room visitor's sign-in sheet.

MIA (*missing...incomplete assignment*): a popular excuse for skipping class on the project due date.

mid-term: the semester checkpoint.

mid-term crisis: the realization that you have ½ a semester left to learn all of the material.

mid-term(s): semi-final exam(s).

minor: anyone drinking who is not of legal age.

miscellaneous: the category under which most of a student's spending money goes.

Monday (*Mon.*): day 1 of classes for the week and the furthest day away from the weekend.

money: paper or plastic.

monotone: the droning voice with which some professors lull their class to sleep.

mouse pad: an off campus apartment with a rodent problem.

multiple choice: eenie, meanie, minie, moe…

multi-task: how to study for 2 or more exams scheduled on the same day.

Murphy's Law: why there's a surprise quiz on the one day that you didn't do the reading.

-N-

nap: to rest ones eyes for a few minutes.

napster: a student renown for taking naps.

night owl: an insomniac.

night school (aka *evening classes*): college after dark.

9mm (*nine more minutes*): the exact amount of extra sleep you get in between alarms.

non-fiction: a true story.

NOTA (*none of the above*): a guess as good as any when you don't know the answer on a multiple-choice question.

notebook: a personal study guide.

notes (aka *class notes*): highlights of the professor's lectures.

note taking: student dictation.

noteworthy: anything that is likely to appear on the exam.

novel: an original idea.

-O-

office hours: designated visitation time with your professor.

online: when you've followed your outline to a 'T.'

online degree: a diploma that you can download yourself.

online education: home schooling.

open: class registration status…good seating still available.

open book exam: the least your professor could do considering how expensive the textbook was.

oral exam: how students are graded in a public speaking course.

orientation: getting to know your way around campus.

osmosis: your only hope of learning the material if you fall asleep while studying.

outline: a written plan of how you're actually going to complete the assignment.

out of state: college far away from home.

outspoken: to lose a debate.

overanalyze: to think way too long and much too hard about something.

overdue: the notice you received from the library regarding the book you borrowed.

overload: enrolling into more courses than you can handle.

overpass: doing extra credit work for a pass/fail course.

oversleep: what you are always in danger of once you turn off the alarm.

over study: to prepare for a quiz as if it were a final exam.

-P-

P: the preferred grade for a pass/fail course.

page requirement: the difference between an essay and a term paper.

paper: a routine writing assignment.

paperback: the cheaper version of a book.

parent weekend: a scheduled family reunion on campus.

partial credit: better than nothing.

part-time: a casual approach to earning a degree.

party animal: the campus mascot.

party school: where clowns earn their degrees.

pass: 60% or better.

Pass/Fail: the difference between earning credit and not.

pay per view: the cost to audit a course.

peer group: whichever clique you're affiliated with.

peer pressure: the drive to maintain grades comparable to your friends…or be ridiculed.

pen: the preferred writing utensil.

pencil: the No.2 preferred writing utensil.

penmanship: the courtesy of returning a borrowed pen at the end of class.

pen pal: the classmate who has an extra pen for you to use.

personal computer: whichever PC you happen to be using in the computer center.

pet peeve: something you disliked long before your roommate started doing it.

philosophy: a thinking man's major.

photocopy: how to get the notes without writing them down.

physical education: getting a workout from carrying your books around.

plagiarism: a conscious decision to not use quotation marks.

plan A: your intent to ace the exam/assignment.

plan B: your hope of earning at least a good grade if plan A doesn't work out.

pledge: a new semester' resolution to study more than you did last term.

PM (*Post Monday*): the "Monday night blues" in anticipation of attending classes the rest of the week.

political science: understanding the differences between Democrats, Republicans and Independents.

pop quiz: an impromptu test to see who did the reading assignment.

pop-ups: surprise quizzes.

postponement: a reprieve from having to take the test today.

power nap: the 1–2 hours of sleep you got after studying through most of the night.

practice test: a prelude to the real deal.

pre-law: leaving a rowdy party before the campus police arrive.

pre-requisite: what you need to know before taking a class.

presentation: show and tell.

print: your most legible handwriting.

printer: anyone who dislikes writing in cursive.

procrastinate: to put off until the last minute.

procrastinator: someone who routinely puts off until tomorrow what should've already been done.

proctor: the timekeeper overseeing the exam.

professional student: someone who studies to the 'nth' degree.

professor: the class key note speaker.

professor profile: feedback from someone who has already taken the professor's class.

project: an authorized collaboration between 2 or more classmates.

proof read: getting a second opinion of your paper...before you pass it in.

pssst: the universal in class cat call.

psyched: a student majoring in psychology.

PTSD (*Post Test Stress Disorder*): a student's high anxiety in anticipation of grades being posted.

punctuation mark: a big, fat, red D.

-Q-

Q&A (*questions & answers*): designated class time during which the professor goes over the graded exam.

quad: a high student occupancy dorm room.

question: that which requires an answer.

question mark: to challenge the accuracy of your grade.

quiz: a mini-test.

quotation marks: how not to plagiarize.

quote: a memorable saying by someone famous.

-R-

R&R (*reading & writing*): doing schoolwork.

read: your homework assignment.

reading period: the few days preceding an exam.

real world: life after college.

reboot: ctrl, alt, del.

recycle: to redeem your books for money at the end of the semester.

refresher course: any class scheduled after a gruelingly boring one.

register: to officially reserve your seat in a class(es).

registrar: the keeper of all records at a college.

registrar's office: the library of all student records.

registration: documented proof that you're enrolled in classes.

registration fee: a surcharge on documenting that you're enrolled in classes.

remedial classes: correspondence courses.

report card: your semester transcript.

required reading: all of the material that you'll be tested on.

requirements: all that you need to know en route to earning your degree.

re-read: another attempt to understand material that you already read.

reschedule: to exercise the add/drop option.

research: exhausting all resources until you've got enough information to write a paper.

research paper: a well documented report.

reserves: the read-only section of the library.

residence hall: a dorm named in honor of a generous donor to the college.

residence life: dorm living.

resident assistant: a dorm manager in training.

resident director: the dorm manager.

retake: an exam 'do-over'.

review: to refresh one's memory.

review session: the last chance before an exam to identify which notes you're missing.

review sheet: the last hand-out given before the exam.

revised: the new and improved version of your paper.

rewrite: take two.

rhetorical question: whatever the professor asked the class and no one raised their hand to answer.

right: the answer with a checkmark next to it.

RIP (*read in peace*): the library motto.

rollover: step two in your morning wake-up routine.

roll over minutes: sleep time after you hit the snooze button.

room & board: the cost of living on campus.

roommate(s): the other student(s) with a key to your dorm room.

rough draft: your first edition of a paper.

RRR (*the 3 R's*): reading, writing and rewriting.

rush: the end result of waiting until the last minute.

rush chair: the last available seat in an overcrowded classroom.

rush week: the last 7 days you have before a deadline.

-S-

safety school: any college which when accepted you can actually afford to attend.

save: to hold a seat in class for your friend.

scan: to browse the material with no intention of really reading it.

schedule: when you're suppose to be in class.

scheduling: the skillful pursuit to coordinate the optimal selection of classes and class times.

scheduling conflict: 2 popular classes offered at the same time.

scholar: anyone in good academic standing.

scholarship: a tuition voucher.

school newspaper: the campus circular.

school supplies: course materials.

school work: employment at the college.

school year: 2 semesters.

seating plan: to avoid the front row.

second class: your first class of the day if you oversleep.

second guess: another answer which may or may not be better than the first one you wrote down.

section(s): a class(es) within a class.

semester: the 15–18 weeks that you have to learn the material.

seminar: an intimate learning environment.

senior: the elder statesman on campus.

senior-itis: a 4th year students' defense for lacking desire to do any work.

senior year: the last hurrah.

shhhh: a polite way to say: "Be quiet, I'm trying to study."

short-term: a summer session.

short-term memory: forgetting everything studied the minute the exam is over.

single: a dorm room for the student who doesn't like to share.

single sex college: his or her school.

single sex dorm: his or her housing.

single space: no room to read between the lines.

slacker: a student majoring in minimalism.

sleeper: a student who requires a minimum of 8 hours rest per night.

sleep study: watching other students fall asleep in class.

sleepwalk: the trance-like state in which students make their way to early morning classes.

SMAC (*see me after class*): an impromptu meeting called by your professor.

snooze: the large, easy to find in your sleep, alarm reset button on your clock.

snooze button: step one in your morning wake-up routine.

social policy: a campus guide to having fun.

social science: the art of making friends and influencing people.

social life: having things to do and friends to do them with...other than study.

sophomore: an accomplished freshman.

sophomore jinx: a superstition often used to justify a 2nd year students' drop in gpa.

sophomore year: your second tour of duty on campus.

sophomoric: a step above freshman-esque.

sorority: an exclusive girls only club on campus.

sorority house: an exclusive girls only clubhouse on campus.

spam: the mystery meat in the dinning hall.

special education: a degree from an Ivy League school.

speed read: how a procrastinator is able to cover so much material at the last minute.

speed write: how a procrastinator is able to complete a paper at the last minute.

spell check: the lost art of consulting a dictionary.

split decision: guessing on a true/false question.

spring: the 2nd semester of the school year.

spring break: the highlight of the school year.

SRO (*standing room only*): seating availability in a popular course on the first day of classes.

stereo-type: to write a paper while listening to music.

stress: not knowing if you've studied enough.

stress buster: getting an A.

stressed out: knowing that you haven't studied enough.

stress test: a final.

student: anyone actively in pursuit of a degree.

student affairs: who's dating who?

student body: the unknown classmate sitting next to you.

student center: a designated campus hangout.

student government: campus politics.

student groups: organized cliques.

student ID: to recognize familiar faces in a crowded classroom.

student life: 2–3 classes a day, periodic assignments/exams, and the rest of the time to yourself.

student loan: money that you'll be paying back long after you've graduated.

student visa: pretty much the same thing as a student MasterCard.

study: a prerequisite to doing well in school.

study break: the 10–15 minutes that passed when you dozed off while reading.

study group: a meeting of the minds.

study hall: the library.

study partner: a tutor.

subject: the topic of discussion.

substitute: a guest speaker.

Summa cum laude: Latin for "you da man."

summary: an abbreviated version of a story.

summarize: to make a long story short.

summer break: what separates one school year from the next.

summer school: an oxymoron.

sweats (*pants & shirts*): ready-to-wear clothing.

syllabus: a class "to-do" list.

synopsis: a brief overview.

-T-

T (*True*): possibly the wrong answer on a True/False question.

T-time (*test time*): the moment of truth.

TA (*teaching assistant*): a professor wannabe.

tailgate: to stand too close behind someone while waiting in line.

take home exam: a homework assignment worth a large percentage of your final grade.

T&A (*titles & authors*): your bookstore checklist.

TBA (*to be announced*): a course scheduling uncertainty.

technology: why your once state-of-the-art computer is now outdated.

term: a semester.

term paper: a semester long writing assignment.

test: the standard measure of what you have or haven't learned.

test date: the deadline by which you need to know the material.

test site: the laboratory.

textbook: the main source of material on which you'll be tested.

TGIF (*thank God I'm finished*): popular student sentiment upon completing a huge assignment/finals.

thesaurus: your best bet when at a loss for words.

thesis: a major writing assignment.

thinking cap: any one of the many baseball hats in your collection.

third class: your first class of the day if you really oversleep.

third degree: a post Master's plan to return to school.

Thursday (*Thu*): day 4 of classes for the week and the unofficial start of the weekend.

time limit: however long you have to complete the exam.

TLC (*too late...closed*): a registration hazard.

TMI (*too much information*): the difficulty in studying for a cumulative final exam.

tongue tied: not being able to say the words that are right on the tip of your tongue.

topic: what you were assigned to write about.

total enrollment: the number of students who appear in class on the day of the exam.

trademark: wishful thinking upon learning that a classmate got a better grade.

transcript: a cumulative report card.

transfer credits: the difference between enrolling into a new school as a freshman vs. as a sophomore.

transfer student: someone with previous college experience.

triple: a double with an extra student assigned.

True/False (*T/F*): the difference between right and wrong.

Tuesday (*Tue*): day 2 of classes for the week and the second furthest day away from the weekend.

tuition: the college's cover charge.

tuition & fees: the college's cover charge plus tax.

tuition reimbursement: what you should be entitled to if you don't get an education.

tutor: a personal study guide.

tutorial: a private review session.

TV: a video game system monitor.

type: using 2 or more fingers to operate a computer keyboard.

typo (*typographical error*): why you should always spell chick...ah, spell *check*.

-U-

underclassman: an upperclassman in training.

undergraduate: anyone enrolled in college who hasn't yet earned their degree.

undergraduate school: a pre-requisite to graduate school.

underline: to highlight using an ink pen.

underpass: to flunk a Pass/Fail course.

underscore: failure to earn the point total you predicted prior to taking the test.

understudy: not quite ready for the test.

university: a 4 year or more deferment into the real world.

unquote: to plagiarize.

unread: anyone ducking to avoid being called on in class.

up & coming: late, but on your way to class.

upgrade: the successful result of arguing a test answer that was previously marked wrong.

upperclassman: a veteran student on campus.

upper level: higher learning.

up-to-date: having acquired all of the notes for the day(s) that you missed class.

used: the books with discount stickers on them.

user friendly: something so simple that even a freshman can figure it out.

-V-

valedictorian: the head of the class.

video games: a virtual alternative to studying.

virus: a campus epidemic that infects students and/or their computers.

vocabulary: all of the italicized words listed in the text-book.

volunteer: a student who thinks that he/she knows the answer.

-W-

W: a fail-safe grade option.

wait list: a procrastinator's 'to-do' list.

wake-up-call: getting a D on the mid-term.

wall paper: posters for your dorm room.

wannabe: your sentiments upon receiving a C.

wardrobe: the jeans, sweats, t-shirts and baseball caps in your closet.

wasted: your tuition money if you neglect to go to classes.

weak(est) link: the slacker assigned to your group project.

Wednesday (*Wed*): day 3 of classes for the week and 2 days away from the weekend.

weekend (aka *Saturday & Sunday*): what separates one week from the next.

well-read: anyone with a degree in English Literature.

whisper: the volume at which you'd carry on a conversation in the library.

windows: what you find yourself staring out of during a boring class session.

winter break: the school year's intermission.

WIP (*work in progress*): having started, but not yet finished an assignment.

withdraw: a last ditch effort to salvage your semester gpa.

word association: a popular technique to help you remember things you're likely to forget.

work: employment and/or academic responsibilities.

workaholic: a student whose best friends are textbooks.

workbook: a textbook accompaniment...at an additional cost.

workload: the difference between taking 3 classes vs. taking 5 classes.

worksheet: the scrap paper on which you calculate your answers.

work/study: academic synonyms.

wpm (*words per minute*): how fast a professor talks during lectures.

write: to compose your thoughts onto paper...for a grade.

writer's block: anything that distracts you from completing your paper.

wrong: the test answer with an "X" next to it.

www: What class is it? When does it meet? Where is it located?

-X-

X: what marks the spot of a wrong answer.

X-factor: to calculate your test score according to the number of wrong answers.

X-rated: a test grade so poor that you don't want to show anyone.

XXX: beating a classmate in a game of tic-tac-toe.

-Y-

yawn: an unflattering commentary on a professor's lecture.

Yes/No (*Y/N*): the precursor to the multiple-choice question.

-Z-

zero: an incomplete assignment.

ZZZ: a sure sign that your classmate is asleep.

0-595-33743-0